Original title:
The Poet's Craft

Copyright © 2024 Book Fairy Publishing
All rights reserved.

Author: Karoliina Kadakas
ISBN HARDBACK: 978-9916-87-813-2
ISBN PAPERBACK: 978-9916-87-814-9
ISBN EBOOK: 978-9916-87-815-6

Starlit Verses

Under the blanket of night,
Wonders dance in soft light.
Each star tells a tale,
Whispers carried on the gale.

Moonbeams weave through the trees,
Swaying gently with the breeze.
Night's embrace calls softly,
In dreams we wander, lofty.

Silent echoes fill the sky,
As constellations sigh high.
A lover's oath in the dark,
Flickers bright, igniting spark.

Galaxies spin, worlds collide,
In this vastness, we confide.
Time stands still as we dream,
Lost in starlit silver streams.

Let the night cradle our fears,
Hold our hopes, wipe our tears.
With every glance to the heights,
Our souls dance in starlit nights.

A Map of Musings

Wandering thoughts take flight,
Navigating realms of light.
With each twist, a new path,
Exploring joy and wrath.

Across valleys of doubt,
Mountains rise, fears shout.
In whispers of the trees,
Secrets drift on the breeze.

Ink stains mark our trials,
Pages filled with weary smiles.
Through shadows, we will tread,
Past the words left unsaid.

Every line tells a tale,
A compass when we fail.
With hope as our guide,
We'll weather the rising tide.

In the map of heart's terrain,
We'll harvest joy from pain.
With every step, we choose,
In this journey, we can't lose.

The Silent Symphony

In gentle whispers, notes arise,
The wind carries them 'neath starlit skies.
Each heartbeat plays a tender tune,
In quiet corners, dreams commune.

The rustling leaves, a soft refrain,
Nature's music, free from pain.
A melody in every glance,
Life dances softly in a trance.

Echoes linger, sweet and low,
In moments shared, the feelings flow.
Beneath the moon, we find our place,
In silent symphonies of grace.

With every breath, the world awakes,
Harmony in the path it takes.
The universe in perfect sync,
In stillness, we learn to think.

So let us hold this soundless art,
Let it resonate within the heart.
For in the silence, we shall find,
A symphony that speaks all kinds.

Chasing Inked Rainbows

With pen in hand, I chase the light,
In every stroke, a vibrant sight.
Colors blend in fluid streams,
As passions flow in vivid dreams.

Each hue a story waiting there,
A canvas blank, yet full of flair.
The palette spills with joy and pain,
In the pursuit of inked rain.

With every drop, a heart's release,
In whispered words, I find my peace.
Chasing rainbows, bold and bright,
In every shade, a world ignites.

As sunsets fade, new colors bloom,
From every shadow, hope finds room.
The spectrum dances, wild and free,
In inked rainbows, I find me.

So let me gather these moments bright,
With vivid dreams taking flight.
Chasing the colors of my soul,
In every splash, I feel whole.

Sculpting Sentences

Words take shape like clay in hand,
Formed with care across the land.
Each phrase a curve, each thought a line,
In sculpting sentences, we define.

Chiseling the edges, smooth and clear,
A voice emerges, strong and near.
With every word, a story grows,
In the silence, creativity flows.

Crafting meaning with delicate grace,
In every sentence, I find my place.
A literary dance, a nuanced art,
Sculpting thoughts that touch the heart.

As I mold the matter of dreams,
Each letter breathes, or so it seems.
In wordsmithing, I find my truth,
A sculptor's pride, a poet's youth.

So let these sentences stand tall,
In the gallery of life, they call.
A testament to all I've penned,
In sculpted lines, my soul transcends.

Unspoken Histories in Rhyme

In shadows linger tales untold,
Whispers of the brave and bold.
Each silence carries weight and dreams,
Unspoken truths in woven themes.

From ancient roots, the stories rise,
Beneath the stars, beneath the skies.
In every heartbeat, echoes trace,
Histories lost in time and space.

With every rhyme, I seek to weave,
The fabric of what we believe.
Connecting threads both near and far,
In silent songs, we find the star.

Moments captured, yet left unsaid,
In every line, the path we tread.
Unspoken histories softly rhyme,
Remnants of our shared timeline.

So let the verses gently sing,
Of journeys past and what they bring.
In every breath, we find our peace,
In unspoken histories, sweet release.

Sculpting Silence into Sound

In the stillness, whispers grow,
Echoes dance where thoughts may flow.
Carved from dreams, a voice takes flight,
Molding shadows into light.

Each breath a note, soft and clear,
Crafting music we hold dear.
Walls of quiet start to sway,
As silence turns to bright array.

In hidden corners, beauty waits,
A symphony that celebrates.
With gentle hands, we shape the air,
Transforming silence, rich and rare.

Every heartbeat, a steady drum,
Emotions rise, the pulse becomes.
From emptiness, a song does stream,
Sculpting silence into dream.

Listen close, the echoes call,
In this space, we find it all.
With open hearts, we break the ground,
Sculpting silence into sound.

Chisel of the Mind

With thought like stone, I start to shape,
A vision born, an ardent escape.
Fingers steady, resolve so strong,
I carve out wisdom, right from wrong.

Each crack and line tells a tale,
Of battles lost and hopes that sail.
Chiseling through the heavy doubt,
I find the voice within to shout.

Ideas breathe as I create,
From raw potential to a fate.
The chisel moves, my spirit roams,
Crafting a world, a place called home.

Fragments fall, yet form anew,
Every thought, a chance to view.
Through trials faced, I gain the grind,
With passion's tool, the chisel's mind.

What emerges is a work of art,
A fusion of the soul and heart.
Through every stroke, I seek and find,
The beauty formed, the chisel of the mind.

The Canvas of Inspiration

In colors bright, the canvas waits,
To capture dreams, to shift the fates.
Brush in hand, I start to play,
With strokes of hope, I pave the way.

Each hue a voice, a silent shout,
A world imagined, no room for doubt.
Swirling visions come alive,
Inspiration's light begins to thrive.

Textures speak, emotions swell,
In every layer, a story to tell.
From chaos born, a structured frame,
The canvas breathes, it knows my name.

With every line, I break the night,
Into dawn's embrace, a fierce delight.
The journey flows, creation's wave,
A masterpiece I proudly crave.

Settled in the colors' song,
I find a place where I belong.
Within this space, I'll always stay,
The canvas of inspiration's sway.

Fragments of a Heart's Mosaic

Each piece a story, shattered part,
Lies within the canvas of the heart.
Mosaic dreams where hopes collide,
Fragments dance, both fierce and wide.

In every shard, a tale is spun,
Of love that flourished, battles won.
Colors blend, a vivid glow,
From broken paths, new visions flow.

Rebuilding hope with careful grace,
Finding beauty in each trace.
A patchwork journey, stitched with care,
Reflecting the dreams that linger there.

In the chaos, a pattern shines,
Together woven, life aligns.
With every piece, we learn to see,
The heart's mosaic, wild and free.

Celebrate the cracks we wear,
Each fragment holds the depth we share.
In this art of love and loss,
A heart's mosaic, we embrace the cost.

Chronicles in Quatrains

In shadows deep, the stories creep,
Of heroes' past and dreams they keep.
Through whispers lost and echoes found,
A world of tales that knows no bound.

Each chapter turned, a lesson learned,
In ink and time, a fire burned.
The pages turn, the echoes sway,
As hearts remember yesterday.

With every line, a thread unwinds,
Of love and loss, of fates entwined.
The quill in hand, the heart on sleeve,
In written words, we dare believe.

Through quests and trials, bonds are forged,
In every tale, a soul's enlarged.
The ink like blood, the paper skin,
A journey's start, and magic's spin.

In chronicles, our lives we trace,
Each quatrain wrapped in warm embrace.
For whether joy or sorrow we find,
In every verse, we're intertwined.

Wavelengths of Wonder

In gentle waves, the colors blend,
A tapestry of light we send.
Through every hue, a story told,
In wavelengths bright, our hearts unfold.

The sun dips low, the sky ablaze,
In twilight's grasp, a moment stays.
We dance in shades, we laugh and sing,
In wonder's realm, our spirits take wing.

When silent nights and stars collide,
In cosmic whispers, dreams abide.
Each twinkle bright, a hope's embrace,
In vast expanse, we find our place.

Through nature's depths, the wonders swirl,
In every breeze, the leaves unfurl.
From ocean tides to mountain air,
In wavelengths deep, our souls lay bare.

In every glance, a spark ignites,
In shared adventures and starry nights.
Together we create our own,
In wavelengths of wonder, we have grown.

The Alchemist's Script

With gold and stone, the secrets mix,
The alchemist's heart knows ancient tricks.
In shadowed rooms with candles bright,
Transforming dreams into pure light.

The whispered chants, the bubbling brew,
In every drop, a wish comes true.
From base to blessed, a journey long,
In alchemy, we find our song.

Through keys of wisdom, doors unfold,
The mysteries wrapped in tales of old.
With every turn of fate's keen hand,
The alchemist writes across the land.

In crystal vials, the magic stirs,
With every breath, the universe purrs.
From lead to love, with heart and mind,
In scripts of gold, our fate's defined.

Through ancient texts and sacred lore,
The alchemist seeks forevermore.
In every spell, a life reborn,
In scripts of change, we are adorned.

Whirlwind of Words

In flurries swift, the phrases soar,
A whirlwind spins from sea to shore.
Each tale a breeze, each thought a thread,
In currents wild, our voices spread.

With every gust, new stories bloom,
In laughter bright, we chase the gloom.
Within the storm, our hearts will race,
In whirlwinds of words, we find our place.

Through swirling skies and tempests stark,
A lighthouse shines, a guiding spark.
In chaos' dance, we choose to weave,
In every breath, what we believe.

As words take flight, they twist and twine,
In wondrous forms, our spirits shine.
From heart to heart, the echoes flare,
In whirlwind's joy, we breathe the air.

With every spin, our dreams align,
In whirlwinds, love and hope entwine.
Through every storm, we rise and share,
In words we find the world laid bare.

The Heartbeat of Ink

In the quiet of the night,
Words dance upon the page,
Each stroke a silent fight,
A tale that breaks the cage.

Whispers of the soul ignite,
As pen meets paper's embrace,
Drawing shadows into light,
An artful kind of grace.

Moments captured, fears confide,
Inky rivers, thoughts traverse,
Within the scribbles, secrets hide,
A universe in each verse.

The heartbeat echoes strong,
In letters, loves, and dreams,
An anthem, soft yet long,
Life flows through inked streams.

With every line, a truth revealed,
An emotion carved in time,
The hidden heart, once sealed,
Now sings in rhythmic rhyme.

Tapestry of Time

Threads entwined, a gentle weave,
Stories etched in each design,
Moments shared, none can cleave,
A tapestry, so divine.

Colors fade, yet memories stay,
Each stitch a heartbeat's trace,
Woven dreams in bright array,
Patterns form, leave no space.

Seasons shift, but we remain,
In the fabric of our days,
Joy and sorrow, joy and pain,
Stitched through life's countless ways.

With every thread, a tale unfolds,
In the loom of endless night,
A legacy, rich and bold,
A glimpse of radiant light.

Embrace the weave, let it flow,
Through the ages, ever bright,
For in this tapestry, we grow,
A journey spun in twilight.

Brushstrokes of Emotion

A canvas waits, untouched and bare,
Hues collide in joyful chaos,
With each stroke, a breath of air,
Feelings spill, never lost.

Whispers of the heart take form,
As colors swirl in wild dance,
From tender touch to raging storm,
Each brushstroke, a fleeting chance.

Moments captured, frames unite,
In vibrant splashes, life's embrace,
The beauty found in wrong and right,
A masterpiece of time and space.

Layer upon layer, emotions blend,
In palettes rich, shadows loom,
An artist's heart begins to mend,
From chaos, springs forth bloom.

Let the colors speak their truth,
A language pure, no need for sound,
In every stroke, there lies our youth,
Infinite stories to be found.

The Light within the Lines

Hidden glow in whispers bright,
Each line a pathway to the soul,
Through shadows deep, emerges light,
A journey, part of the whole.

In curves and angles, tales unfold,
A geometric dance of fate,
With every stroke, a truth retold,
A rhythm none can negate.

The pen, a wand of flickering fire,
Igniting dreams that long to soar,
Each loop and turn, a heart's desire,
Unlocking pathways, opening doors.

Illumination in the dark,
Each letter holds a spark divine,
In every page, a glowing mark,
A beacon 'midst the confine.

Celebrate the shapes we weave,
For in the lines, our stories shine,
In every heart, a world to believe,
A legacy, profound, aligns.

Tapestry of Thought

Threads of memory weave tight,
Colors blend in borrowed light.
Dreams and fears in shadows play,
A tapestry of night and day.

Wisps of echoes softly dance,
Holding hopes in fragile glance.
Each stitch tells a tale untold,
In patterns bright and shadows bold.

Fingers trace the lines of fate,
Each knot a moment, small but great.
Woven whispers in the air,
A story spun with utmost care.

Through the loom, ideas flow,
In every corner, wonders grow.
Frayed ends beckon, call me near,
A tapestry of love and fear.

With every thread, a voice awakes,
In colored layers, the heart breaks.
A picture painted, bold and deep,
In this tapestry, secrets keep.

Metaphors in Motion

Words dance lightly on the page,
Painting visions, free from cage.
Each symbol breathes a life anew,
In rhythms vast, in hues of blue.

Stories whispered on the breeze,
Carried softly through the trees.
A river flows through heart and soul,
With every word, we lose control.

Time ticks slowly, moments bend,
In verses where the journeys blend.
Metaphors like birds take flight,
Soaring high into the night.

Feelings echo, bright and rare,
Captured in the open air.
Motion paints the silent scene,
A dance of dreams where we have been.

With every step, we find our way,
In the words that come to play.
A symphony of thoughts in bloom,
Metaphors erase the gloom.

Echoes of Expression

Whispers linger in the light,
Voices drift into the night.
Echoes ripple through the air,
Each sound a thought, a silent prayer.

Lines of feeling stretch and sway,
In every pause, there comes a play.
Emotions surge, then fade away,
Leaving traces in disarray.

Canvas painted with desire,
Brushstrokes tell of heart's own fire.
With every hue, a tale unfolds,
In rich textures, the spirit holds.

Expressions caught, like fleeting light,
Flecks of truth in shadows bright.
Every echo bears a face,
In the silence, we find grace.

Songs of longing, soft and sweet,
Resonate in steady beat.
Echoes whisper, never cease,
In expression, we find peace.

From Silence to Stanza

In quiet depths, ideas bloom,
From silence born, they find their room.
A gentle pulse, a heart laid bare,
Crafting words with tender care.

Each stanza builds a bridge to light,
A journey woven through the night.
In every line, a heartbeat strong,
Transforming whispers into song.

The quietude holds secrets vast,
In stillness, chains of doubt are cast.
From nothing blooms a vivid thread,
In silence, every fear is shed.

Words emerge as stars align,
Bringing forth the divine design.
In cadence soft, their dances sway,
From silence, life finds its way.

Embrace the still, allow it space,
To shape the thoughts we dare to chase.
From silence crafted, beauty flows,
In every stanza, the heart knows.

Sonnet's Secret

In shadows deep where whispers dwell,
A hidden rhyme begins to swell.
With every word, a heart does soar,
Unlocking doors to love's grand lore.

The verses weave like threads of gold,
Tales of passion, gently told.
Each quatrain holds a silent plea,
Yearning souls, forever free.

Time dances lightly on the page,
As ink spills out, we turn the stage.
With every line, hearts intertwine,
In sonnet's secret, love does shine.

Beneath the stars, the poets sigh,
Their dreams take flight, they learn to fly.
In meter's grasp, they find their muse,
A timeless bond that cannot lose.

So let the sonnet's secret grow,
In sweet surrender, let love flow.
For in each verse, a truth revealed,
The heart's desire, forever healed.

The Dance of Syntax

In sentence sway, the words align,
A rhythm born from thought divine.
Each subject pairs with verb and noun,
The dance begins, we spin around.

Adjectives in colors bright,
Illuminate the dark of night.
With every clause, a twist and turn,
A playful spark, a flame we burn.

Punctuation marks, our guiding star,
In every pause, we travel far.
The syntax sings a song so sweet,
In harmony, our souls do meet.

Conjunctions bind, as thoughts unfold,
A narrative in layers told.
In every line, a breath is drawn,
The dance of syntax carries on.

So come, let's play with words today,
In swirling forms, we'll find our way.
With language's dance, our spirits rise,
A jubilee of endless skies.

Palette of Emotions

Colors blend on canvas wide,
Each hue a feeling, deep inside.
The brush of fate creates a scene,
Where joy and sorrow dance between.

A splash of red, a heart exposed,
In vivid strokes, life's truth composed.
With blues that echo in the night,
We find our peace, in shadows light.

The yellow sun brings hope anew,
While softest pink conveys what's true.
In every shade, a story told,
A palette rich, where hearts unfold.

Through strokes of love, the canvas breathes,
With every tear, the spirit weaves.
Emotions captured, framed in time,
A masterpiece in every rhyme.

So paint your world with fervent hues,
In every choice, your heart's own muse.
With colors deep, let feelings flow,
In life's grand art, forever grow.

Illuminated by Language

In word-lit paths, our minds explore,
With every phrase, we seek for more.
The tales of old, alive today,
In language bright, we find our way.

A whisper soft, a thunderous shout,
Each voice, a bridge, connecting doubt.
In every letter, worlds collide,
Illuminated minds abide.

Metaphors like stars align,
In every thought, a spark, a sign.
With stories shared, we journey far,
Together, we become a star.

The language flows like rivers wide,
In every current, truths abide.
Unraveling meaning, searching deep,
In words, our dreams are ours to keep.

So let us speak in colors bright,
For language holds a wondrous light.
In every verse, a spark ignites,
Illuminated by our flights.

Weaving Whimsy

In the twilight glow, dreams entwine,
Colors collide, a dance divine.
Laughter echoes, soft and sweet,
Fantasy blossoms at our feet.

Threads of joy in the gentle air,
Whispers of secrets, sweet and rare.
Imagination's quilt, so bright,
Woven patterns in soft light.

Threads of Narration

Words like rivers flow and bend,
Carrying tales that never end.
Each stitch a story, rich and deep,
In the fabric of dreams, we leap.

Characters born from threads of gold,
Adventures waiting to unfold.
A tapestry of life's embrace,
In every corner, a hidden place.

Untold Stories on Paper

Pages whisper, secrets confined,
Ink spills truths, hearts intertwined.
Silent voices yearn to speak,
Hidden gems in every week.

A canvas waiting, pure and bright,
To capture shadows, give them light.
Each line a portal to the past,
Stories waiting to be cast.

A Journey of Lines

With every stroke, a path is traced,
A dance of curves, no step misplaced.
In the journey, we find our way,
Through winding roads in shades of gray.

Lines collide, a vibrant mix,
Each twist reveals a new fix.
Adventure calls with every line,
In the artistry, our souls align.

Woven with Feeling

In the quiet corners we find,
Threads of emotion intertwined.
Hopes like fabric, soft and bright,
Crafted gently, day and night.

Whispers linger in the air,
Stories woven with tender care.
Hearts unfold like silken blooms,
In this tapestry that looms.

Colors dancing, shadows play,
Reflections of dreams that sway.
Every heartbeat leaves a mark,
Within this canvas, light and dark.

Through the textures, we embrace,
Moments stitched in time and space.
Every thread a tale to tell,
In this woven world we dwell.

With every knot, our lives entwine,
Crafting paths that brightly shine.
Through love's fibers, we shall weave,
A masterpiece we'll never leave.

Castles Built of Verse

In the realm where words take flight,
Castles rise in the soft twilight.
Brick by brick, with careful thought,
Each line a treasure, nobly sought.

Turrets tall, with banners high,
Stories echo, reaching the sky.
Rhymes like starlight, shining bold,
In every verse, a world unfolds.

Windows framed with metaphors,
Open wide to distant shores.
Within these walls, a heart's refrain,
Resonates through joy and pain.

Battlements of slender dreams,
Guarded by the poet's themes.
Each stanza holds a fierce desire,
Igniting souls with woven fire.

In this kingdom, we shall dwell,
Crafted by the words we tell.
Castles built with passion's pen,
Forever standing, time and again.

Empires of Imagery

Vast horizons stretch before,
Imagery rich, forevermore.
Mountains rise with every line,
Seas of color, pure divine.

Visions paint the skies anew,
Dreams ignited, bright and true.
Through the brush of words we wield,
Realms of wonder are revealed.

Every detail vividly sings,
Bringing forth majestic things.
In the landscapes of our mind,
Infinite treasures we will find.

Starlit paths and sunlit ways,
Guide us through the endless days.
Within this empire, we shall roam,
Finding beauty, heart, and home.

With imagination as our guide,
We shall build where dreams abide.
Empires made with vivid dreams,
Crafting futures, or so it seems.

Dialogues with the Muse

In shadows deep, the muse appears,
Whispering truths to calm our fears.
Words exchanged in sacred space,
Creating magic, time and place.

With gentle nudges, passions rise,
In every thought, the heart complies.
Crafting verses, line by line,
In this dance, our souls entwine.

Questions linger in the air,
Sparks of genius, beyond compare.
Together we explore the night,
Illuminated by the light.

Each response a treasure found,
Echoes of thoughts that swirl around.
In this dialogue, clear and true,
The muse and poet break anew.

Through every word, connection blooms,
In harmony, the spirit zooms.
A sacred bond, so strong and bright,
Dialogues that fill the night.

Alighting on a Page

Ink drops fall like gentle rain,
Whispers woven in soft refrain.
Thoughts take flight on wings of grace,
Each word finding its destined place.

Beneath the pen, emotions flow,
Stories rise where shadows grow.
In every curve, a tale unfolds,
Life's secrets captured, quietly told.

Lines connect like stars at night,
Illuminating dreams in bright.
Every stanza, a heartbeat's pause,
Revealing truth without a cause.

Fingers dance, a silent muse,
Crafting worlds with every choose.
A canvas built from heart and ink,
Transporting souls to realms we think.

So let your thoughts find open air,
On pages where reflections stare.
For in the quiet, voices play,
Alighting softly on a page.

Breath of the Written Word

In the stillness, whispers call,
Every story holds a thrall.
Pages turn with gentle sighs,
Unfolding dreams beneath the skies.

Words breathe life, they leap and dance,
Capture moments, seize their chance.
From the depths, a voice will rise,
Echoing truth that never lies.

With every stroke, the heart aligns,
Creating rhythms, sacred signs.
Breath of life within each line,
A universe, both yours and mine.

Ink-stained fingers find their way,
Guided by what words can say.
Imagination's sweet embrace,
Leads us to a boundless space.

Let us linger in this glow,
Where the written whispers flow.
In the silence, find your word,
Feel the warmth of love inferred.

Sonorous Strings of Expression

Strummed like strings on an old guitar,
Each note plucked shines like a star.
Harmony in every thought,
Melodies that time forgot.

Echoes resonate through the night,
Carried softly in the light.
Verses bloom like fragrant flowers,
Filling up the quiet hours.

Voices rise, a chorus fair,
Creating magic in the air.
Rhythmic pulses, heartbeats meld,
In the silence, stories held.

Every line a voice unleashed,
Sonorous gifts, a feast increased.
From depths unknown, emotions pour,
Unlocking dreams, forevermore.

Let the music guide your pen,
Orchestrate the thought again.
In the symphony of the mind,
True expression we shall find.

Threads of Thought

Weaver's hand spins tales so fine,
Intricate webs of heart and line.
Threads of gold, silver, and hue,
Telling stories both fresh and new.

Each thought stitched with careful care,
A tapestry rich, beyond compare.
Patterns swirl in playful dance,
Inviting every soul to glance.

In the loom, reflections merge,
Ideas surge like ocean's urge.
Fingers trace the paths they weave,
Crafting dreams that we believe.

Colors bright, or muted tones,
Speak of joys and ancient groans.
With every thread, a connection found,
In the fabric where hopes abound.

So gather 'round this woven space,
Share your threads, embrace their grace.
For in the weaving, truths are wrought,
Life's lovely fabric—threads of thought.

Capturing Fleeting Thoughts

Whispers dance upon the breeze,
Silent echoes of lost dreams.
Moments flicker, quickly fade,
Trapped in time, a fleeting shade.

Catching glimmers of the past,
In the shadows, memories cast.
Each thought a firework's glow,
Bright and brief, then gone, we know.

Chronicles of fleeting light,
Captured in the stillness of night.
Waves of wonder sweep the mind,
In these currents, truth we find.

Every heartbeat tells a tale,
In the whispers, dreams set sail.
Through the chaos, we must sift,
Finding meaning in each gift.

A canvas blank, waiting wide,
For the brush of thoughts to glide.
In the silence, insights bloom,
A dance of colors in the gloom.

The Rhythm of Reflection

In the stillness, thoughts align,
Echoes of a moment's sign.
Each heartbeat marks a gentle chime,
Guiding us through the folds of time.

Ripples surge in quiet pools,
Beneath the surface, wisdom schools.
Ripened thoughts like autumn leaves,
Turning shades as memory weaves.

The pulse of life, a steady beat,
Steps we dance on paths discreet.
Finding grace in shadows cast,
In the present, greet the past.

Voices whisper through the air,
Secrets woven, laid so bare.
With every breath, we draw the line,
In the rhythm, we intertwine.

Glimmers caught in twilight's hue,
Reflecting all that we once knew.
In the mirror, moments blend,
The rhythm of the soul transcends.

Enigma of Emotion

What lies beneath the veil of sighs?
A labyrinth of twisted ties.
Feelings swirl like autumn wind,
An enigma where we begin.

Love and loss, a tight embrace,
Each tear and smile, a fleeting trace.
Colors clash within the heart,
A canvas torn yet set apart.

Unspoken words in silence dwell,
In every heartbeat, stories swell.
Moments grasped in fleeting light,
The dance of shadows in the night.

Beneath the surface, whispers rise,
A symphony of unshed cries.
In the storm, we find our way,
Through the chaos, come what may.

Emotions ebb like waves on shore,
Crashing softly, yearning for more.
In the depth, we seek the key,
To unlock our mystery.

Fragments in Flight

Scattered dreams like autumn leaves,
Fleeting moments, time deceives.
In the air, they twist and twine,
Echoes of a life divine.

Bright stardust falls from skies,
Carrying whispers, soft goodbyes.
Scattered paths we chase in vain,
In the distance, echoes remain.

Time-a thief, so sly and bold,
Stealing treasures, tales untold.
In the currents, fragments fly,
Mapping journeys that we vie.

A kaleidoscope of memories spins,
Dancing to the tune within.
Each shard a piece of who we are,
In every glint, our wish, our star.

Through the air, we softly glide,
Following dreams that will not hide.
In fragments found, we stitch and weave,
A tapestry of all we believe.

The Heart's Lyric

In whispered tones, love speaks,
A gentle breeze, it seeks.
With every beat, a song,
Where souls connect, belong.

Through moonlit nights we roam,
In dreams, we find our home.
A dance beneath the stars,
True affection, never far.

Each moment's soft embrace,
A time, a cherished place.
In echoes of the past,
The heart's lyric, made to last.

In laughter's warm delight,
And shadows kissed by light.
With every tear, we grow,
In love's sweet undertow.

So here we weave our tale,
In colors bold and pale.
A melody of dreams,
The heart's song, endless themes.

Gardens of Rhyme

In gardens lush, thoughts bloom,
Where silence replaces gloom.
With petals soft and bright,
Inspiring joy and light.

Each word a fragrant rose,
From roots where feeling grows.
With verses rich and deep,
In rhymes, our secrets keep.

The sun will kiss the leaves,
As tenderness believes.
Among the vines we find,
A harmony entwined.

Soft whispers fill the air,
Like blooms beyond compare.
In every fragrant line,
A garden's gift divine.

Together hand in hand,
We wander through this land.
With rhythmic steps we tread,
In gardens where love's fed.

A Canvas of Feelings

On canvas vast and wide,
Emotions gently glide.
With colors fierce and bold,
Our stories will unfold.

Each stroke, a heart laid bare,
In blues of deep despair.
And golden hues of morn,
In silence, art is born.

From shadows, we create,
In brilliance, we escape.
With brushes dipped in dreams,
Life's canvas brightly gleams.

A splash of fiery red,
For all the words unsaid.
In every shade we find,
A truth of heart and mind.

So paint with joy and pain,
In colors of the rain.
A masterpiece unique,
In feelings that we seek.

Melody in Metaphor

In music soft and clear,
A universe draws near.
Each note a whispered sigh,
In rhythm, hearts will fly.

With metaphors that sing,
Life's melodies take wing.
A symphony of dreams,
Where hope and love redeems.

A dance of light and shade,
In harmony, we wade.
The chorus of the soul,
In verses, we are whole.

With violins that weep,
In secrets that we keep.
The lyrics paint the view,
In echoes sweet and true.

So let the music flow,
As stars begin to glow.
In metaphor, we dwell,
A story we will tell.

Sculpting Shadows in Stanzas

In twilight's brush, we carve the night,
With whispers soft, our dreams take flight.
The shadows dance, a fleeting gleam,
In every verse, we find our theme.

Beneath the moon, our thoughts collide,
As ink cascades, we cannot hide.
Each strophe sings of silent fears,
Eclipsed by hope, we shed our tears.

A gentle hand shapes every line,
In darkness found, our voices shine.
We pen the stories yet untold,
In stanzas rich, our hearts unfold.

With every pause, a breath of muse,
In sculpted words, we choose to lose.
The echoes blend, the past and now,
In shadowed art, we take a bow.

Together we weave, a tapestry,
Of shadows cast, of light set free.
With every verse, we bridge the gap,
In sculpting shadows, we close the map.

The Canvas Awaits

Beneath the stars, the canvas lies,
An open heart, a thousand skies.
With strokes of fate, we paint it free,
A masterpiece of what can be.

Each hue unveils a hidden dream,
In shadows deep, we find the seam.
A brush in hand, we dare to start,
To craft the world, to mend the heart.

Silent promises in every shade,
A dance of light, a serenade.
From gentle blues to fiery reds,
In every stroke, our heart's thread spreads.

The colors meld, a symphony,
With whispered hopes, we set them free.
Upon the canvas, stories sway,
In every line, our spirits play.

So let us paint till dawn's first light,
With shadows soft and visions bright.
For in this art, we find our place,
The canvas waits; let's fill its space.

Chasing Shadows with Words

In the quiet night, whispers flee,
Chasing shadows, just you and me.
The words we weave become our guide,
In every tale, our dreams collide.

With ink as compass, we roam the dark,
Each letter a flicker, a tiny spark.
From whispered thoughts, the story blooms,
In hidden corners, love resumes.

We chase the echoes of our youth,
In rhymes we seek a deeper truth.
With every stanza, shadows yield,
A place where hope and dreams are healed.

Each syllable, a dance of light,
In chasing shadows of the night.
With every word, we find our way,
To brighter paths, to a new day.

In language sweet, we paint our fears,
With every line, we shed our tears.
Chasing shadows, the heart's embrace,
In words we wander, find our place.

Letters as Landscapes

In written lines, horizons rise,
Letters form where silence lies.
Each word a hill, a valley low,
In landscapes forged where feelings flow.

Beneath the ink, the rivers run,
A journey shared, two hearts as one.
With strokes of thought, we carve the scene,
In landscapes vast, where dreams convene.

Mountains echo with our fears,
In letters penned, we shed our tears.
The roads we travel, both near and far,
In every phrase, a guiding star.

The beauty of our written past,
In landscapes drawn, forever cast.
With each quill's touch, we shape and mold,
In letters bold, our stories told.

From valleys deep to skies so wide,
In letters formed, we cannot hide.
So let the ink flow, the journey start,
For letters as landscapes, speak from the heart.

Harmonies of a Hidden Soul

In the silence where shadows sway,
Melodies whisper, night and day.
Hidden thoughts in gentle streams,
Softly flowing like forgotten dreams.

Beneath the surface, the heart beats slow,
Carrying secrets only silence know.
A rhythm dances, lost in light,
Yearning for truth, embracing the night.

In quiet corners, echoes arise,
Filling the dark with muted sighs.
The soul's song, a fragile thread,
Weaving tales of what lies ahead.

Voices blend in a sweet allure,
As whispers pulse, both tender and sure.
In solitude, a symphony grows,
A hidden world that the spirit knows.

Cradled in doubt, yet bold and bright,
The harmonies bloom in the pale moonlight.
Beneath the calm, the tempest swells,
In the heart of silence, a story dwells.

Prism of Perception

Through the glass, the colors shift,
Reality bends, and time drifts.
Each hue a story, a tale untold,
Casting shadows in shades of gold.

Perception dances, mind takes flight,
Every angle sparks new insight.
Fragments illuminate the unseen,
A world less ordinary, sharp and keen.

In reflections, visions collide,
Chasing dreams we choose to ride.
With every glance, a truth unveiled,
In the spectrum, where souls once sailed.

Layers of meaning, deeper we see,
Every moment, a chance to be free.
Through the prism, the heart reveals,
Life's rich tapestry, its vibrant feels.

In the spectrum's light, we find our place,
Connected through time and timeless grace.
Every shade, a whisper, a scream,
In the prism of perception, we dream.

Architect of Dreams

In the stillness, plans take flight,
Blueprints drawn in the hush of night.
Visions crafted with care and grace,
A vast expanse, an open space.

Foundations firm, with hope infused,
Every heartbeat, a path they used.
Within the mind, the castle glows,
A wondrous realm where creativity flows.

Rooms adorned with thoughts so bright,
Walls echo laughter, pure delight.
Each window framed with endless skies,
A sanctuary where the spirit flies.

Stairways winding, leading to light,
Each step a dream within the flight.
Designs of courage, built on trust,
An architect's vision, bold and just.

Adorned with colors of heart's embrace,
Every corner holds a warm space.
In the heart's blueprints, we find our rhyme,
An architect of dreams, defying time.

Echoes from the Abyss

Whispers surge from the deep unknown,
Echoes linger, in silence sown.
Voices of ages, lost yet clear,
The abyss beckons, do we dare near?

Shadows writhe where fears reside,
In the darkness, memories hide.
Ripples of laughter, a haunting call,
An ancient tale, a rise, a fall.

Starlight flickers, hope's faint gleam,
Through the void, we chase the dream.
Each echo carries a timeless plea,
In the depths, what will we see?

Courage stirs from the depths' embrace,
Seeking solace in the dark space.
As we wander through the haunting mist,
In echoes' arms, we find our tryst.

From the abyss, the heart draws near,
In shadows' grip, there's nothing to fear.
In the stillness, we rise and sing,
Gathering echoes, the pain they bring.

Whispered Verses

Softly spoken words take flight,
Carving shadows in the night.
A gentle breeze, a fleeting thought,
Secrets linger in the wrought.

Each whisper spins a tale anew,
Of joys embraced and dreams that grew.
In quiet corners, truths unwind,
Lost echoes we are yet to find.

When silence wraps its velvet cloak,
Every glance, each breath we stoke.
Together, here, we weave our fate,
In whispered verses, hearts elate.

A dance of words that softly sway,
In the stillness, we wish to stay.
For in each whisper lies a spark,
Illuminating all the dark.

So let us speak without a sound,
In sacred spaces, love is found.
With whispered verses, hand in hand,
In silence, together we stand.

Labyrinths of Language

In the maze where meanings drift,
Words weave paths, a subtle gift.
Twisting phrases, shadowed light,
Voices calling through the night.

Every corner hides a clue,
A labyrinth for me and you.
The echoes dance in endless space,
Chasing whispers, finding grace.

In riddles locked, we search for truth,
Lost in the stories of our youth.
A turn, a twist, the way to find,
The heart's desire, intricately designed.

With every step, a chance to grow,
In language lost, we reap what's sown.
Each turn reveals a hidden song,
In the labyrinth where we belong.

So guide me through these woven lines,
In tangled thoughts, our fate entwines.
Together we'll make sense of the maze,
In the labyrinth of language, we'll blaze.

Mosaic of Metaphor

Shattered colors, pieces bright,
Craft a story in the light.
Each fragment holds a hidden truth,
In the art of a timeless youth.

A metaphor paints the night sky,
Where the dreams of poets lie.
In scattered forms, we find our voice,
In every shard, a whispered choice.

With every hue, a different tale,
Woven softly, never pale.
Mosaics of thoughts in every heart,
Together forming a complex art.

Let us gather what is broken,
In language sweetly left unspoken.
For in the chaos lies the peace,
A mosaic of metaphor, our release.

So craft with me this vivid scene,
From every shade, a world unseen.
In this artwork of heart and mind,
The essence of our souls, combined.

Logos and Lyricism

In words, we find the spark of light,
Logos shines, a guiding sight.
Yet in the rhythm, lyric flows,
Where deeper wisdom gently grows.

Crafting logic with a heart's embrace,
In every stanza, we find our place.
The dance of reason, passion's song,
In symphony, we all belong.

Let ideas blend with artful grace,
In every verse, a sacred space.
For logic grounded in the soul,
Brings clarity to make us whole.

Together, through these lines we weave,
A tapestry few can conceive.
Logos and lyricism entwine,
In every heartbeat, they align.

So let us ponder, let us dream,
Amidst the echoes of the theme.
In words, we chart the stars above,
Through logos and lyrical love.

The Architecture of Emotion

In shadows deep, where feelings dwell,
Each heartbeat echoes like a bell.
Walls of joy, ceilings of pain,
A structure built from love and rain.

Windows open to the soul's vast view,
Each frame a glimpse of what is true.
Bridges of laughter, corridors wide,
In this space, we cannot hide.

Foundations laid by dreams we chase,
A blueprint drawn from time and space.
Rooms adorned with whispered fears,
A gallery of hopes, and silent tears.

Staircases spiraling to the sky,
Each step a reason, a question why.
This house of hearts, an endless song,
Where every emotion has a home, belong.

So let us wander, let us roam,
Through this architecture, find our home.
In every corner, let us see,
The beauty of our shared history.

Where Words Find Wings

In whispered thoughts, our spirits soar,
Each word a key, unlocking doors.
With ink and quill, we sketch the skies,
Crafting tales where silence flies.

Sentences dance like fireflies bright,
Reflecting dreams in the cloak of night.
Pages flutter with a gentle breeze,
As verses echo among the trees.

In every stanza, a heartbeat found,
Words take flight where souls abound.
Through tangled lines and rhymes we weave,
Stories born for hearts to believe.

A chorus rising from deep within,
Where sorrows fade and joys begin.
With every letter, we break the cage,
And let our voices become the stage.

So let the words take wing and fly,
Beyond the limits of the sky.
In every language, our dreams align,
For in those words, the stars will shine.

Palette of Silent Stories

Colors whisper on the canvas bare,
Each stroke a tale, vivid and rare.
Shades of longing, hues of regret,
A masterpiece none can forget.

Textures layered, emotions blend,
In silent stories, hearts transcend.
Brushes dancing, capturing time,
A visual song, a rhyme sublime.

Every drop tells of love's embrace,
In vibrant tones, we find our place.
While shadows linger in corners unseen,
They hold the secrets of what has been.

From dusk till dawn, the palette shifts,
A spectrum blooming in soulful gifts.
Through eyes of silence, we begin to see,
The beauty in our shared history.

So let us paint with passion's fire,
A symphony of colors that never tire.
In every silence, stories reveal,
The artistry of what we feel.

Tides of Imagery

Waves crash softly on the shore,
Each splash a story, a memory's lore.
The ocean breathes in a rhythmic way,
Pulling us close, then drifting away.

Sand slips through fingers, time's cruel game,
A timeless dance, yet never the same.
In every tide, a vision's bloom,
Carried by whispers, a lover's tune.

Seashells hold secrets of journeys past,
Stories of hopes and dreams that last.
Reflections shimmering in the light,
Capturing shadows that wander in flight.

Clouds drift overhead, painting the air,
Sketching the dreams we all may share.
With every surge, the heartbeats rise,
A chorus sung beneath soft skies.

So let the tides of our minds collide,
In waves of imagery, let us ride.
For in each ebb, a new thought's born,
In this ocean of life, we are reborn.

Dance of the Diction

Words waltz in a gentle breeze,
Whispers rise like dancing leaves.
They twirl on pages, soft and bright,
In rhythm with the heart's delight.

Crafted tales in evening's glow,
A symphony of thoughts that flow.
Each stanza striking a perfect chord,
In this dance, we're never bored.

From silence springs a vibrant sound,
In every line, new worlds are found.
Emotion painted on each face,
In this dance, we find our place.

Swaying slowly, the words align,
Crafting stories, divine design.
An orchestra of silent charms,
In the dance, the soul disarms.

So let us spin in word's embrace,
Together lost in time and space.
For in the dance of diction true,
A universe awaits for you.

Threads of Time and Tongue

We weave our tales across the years,
With golden threads and silver tears.
Moments stitched with tender care,
In every heartbeat, memories share.

Words echo from the dawn of days,
Binding voices in endless ways.
Time's fabric, rich in hue and tone,
In this tapestry, we are not alone.

Each whisper carries centuries past,
In every sigh, a story cast.
Threads connect the now and then,
Through language shared, we dare to blend.

Colors of laughter, shades of pain,
Every thread holds a sweet refrain.
Bound together, we rise and fall,
In the stories we share, we find it all.

Let tongues entwine in vivid ties,
As time unfurls before our eyes.
In this realm where memories cling,
We sing the songs of everything.

Capturing Fleeting Thoughts

Thoughts like fireflies, swift and bright,
Flicker softly in the night.
We reach with nets of words and dreams,
To catch those glimmers, break the seams.

In quiet corners, whispers play,
Each thought a gem that fades away.
With ink and pen, we carve the light,
Preserving moments, pure and right.

But like the mist, they slip and sway,
These fleeting thoughts, they will not stay.
A dance of shadows, lost in time,
Yet captured here in silent rhyme.

Through pages worn, our minds ignite,
In swirling depths, we chase the light.
Though thoughts may fade, their essence stays,
In written lines, they weave our ways.

So grasp each thought, hold fast and tight,
For in their glow, we find our sight.
In every captured, whispered breeze,
Life's fleeting moments aim to please.

Radiance in Reflection

Mirrors hold a world so clear,
In stillness, we draw near.
Faces change with every glance,
In reflections, life's dance.

Shadows play on the wall of light,
Echoes whisper soft and bright.
What we see is not the whole,
In every depth, there lies a soul.

Beauty rests in every flaw,
Each mark a story, a silent law.
In time, we learn to embrace,
The radiance of every face.

Glimmers of hope in trials faced,
In reflecting pools, the past is traced.
We find our strength in gentle light,
In mirrored love, we take our flight.

So stand with me by twilight's gleam,
In reflection, we dare to dream.
For in each glance, a truth appears,
Radiance blooms throughout the years.

Revelations in Rhythm

In shadows dance the truths we seek,
Whispers weave through night so bleak.
With every beat, a secret sigh,
Awakening the stars up high.

A pulse of life, a vibrant song,
Echoing where dreams belong.
Each moment holds a hidden grace,
Unraveling in time and space.

From silence springs a radiant glow,
The heart finds peace in what we know.
A rhythm born from deep within,
Where hope ignites and fears grow thin.

Through every struggle, joy will rise,
A symphony beneath the skies.
In measures soft, in tones so bright,
We dance through shadows, into light.

So let the music guide our way,
As revelations come to play.
In every note, a story found,
Resounding love in every sound.

Cadence of the Heart

The heart beats strong, a constant flow,
In rhythm of the love we know.
Gentle whispers in the night,
Carrying dreams that take to flight.

In every glance, a spark ignites,
With passion warming lonely nights.
Together we create a song,
In cadence where we both belong.

The world spins fast, yet here we stand,
Two souls entwined, a bond so grand.
In every breath, a tender grace,
In perfect time, we find our place.

With joys and pains, the music swells,
A tapestry of tales it tells.
With every note, our hearts unite,
In cadence, bliss, and pure delight.

And as the stars begin to fade,
In memories, our love is laid.
The pulse remains, forever near,
In every beat, it's crystal clear.

Ink and Imagination

With ink I weave the tales untold,
In every line, my dreams unfold.
The paper speaks in whispers soft,
Elevating visions, dreams aloft.

Imagination takes its flight,
Through colors bold and words of light.
In every stroke, a world anew,
A canvas rich with vibrant hue.

The quill transforms the night to day,
Unlocking paths where thoughts can play.
In every chapter, life cascades,
As ink spills truth in gentle shades.

Through pages worn, the stories dance,
In every rhythm, a fleeting chance.
With every pen, a universe,
In dreams we roam, the words diverse.

So let the ink flow, wild and free,
For in these pages, find the key.
To unlock worlds we dare to chase,
Creating magic in this space.

Verses in Tapestry

Threads of stories intertwine,
In every verse, a sacred sign.
Woven tales of love and strife,
Binding moments, rich with life.

Each color tells of dreams anew,
In vibrant hues, in shades we view.
A tapestry that time has spun,
Reflecting all that we have done.

Through every knot, a strength revealed,
In scars of losses, hearts have healed.
From fragile threads, we find our voice,
In every stitch, we make our choice.

In laughter shared, in tears we've shed,
The fabric holds the words unsaid.
In unity, we stand as one,
In woven warmth, a life begun.

So let us craft this tale with care,
Each verse a journey that we share.
In tapestry, our lives unfold,
A masterpiece that must be told.

Fragments of a Wandering Mind

Thoughts scatter like leaves in the breeze,
Drifting softly, lost with ease.
A fleeting whisper, a distant sound,
In the chaos, clarity is found.

Paths diverge in a tangled maze,
Echoes linger through the haze.
Questions dance in twilight's glow,
While answers hide beneath the flow.

Fragments merge to form a whole,
Each piece speaks to the heart and soul.
In silence, stories rise and fall,
Wandering minds enchant us all.

Moments frozen, a snapshot view,
Melding dreams with shades of blue.
Chronicles etched in fleeting time,
Wandering thoughts draw a line.

In whispers soft, the journey weaves,
Through tangled roots, through autumn leaves.
A wandering mind finds its way home,
In every fragment, a world to roam.

Architecture of Emotion

Steel and glass against the sky,
Framed by dreams, where feelings lie.
Windows open, revealing the past,
Each corner holds a memory cast.

Walls painted with shadows of pain,
Foundations laid in joy and rain.
Rooms echo laughter, whisper fears,
A structure built of hopes and tears.

Stairs that spiral, lead to heights,
Where aspirations soar like kites.
Balconies that overlook the soul,
In every story, a search for whole.

Underneath the arches of grace,
Emotions find their rightful place.
Blueprints drawn from moments shared,
In the light, we feel prepared.

Each level stacked, a journey vast,
Brick by brick, we hold the past.
In the architecture we create,
Emotions shape our very fate.

Pages Worn by Wisdom

Pages crinkle under gentle hands,
Secrets held in timeless strands.
Wisdom whispers through the ink,
Inviting minds to pause and think.

Chapters filled with trials faced,
Every lesson, love embraced.
A journey of the heart unfolds,
In every story, truth it holds.

Margins speak of dreams foreseen,
Every doodle holds a theme.
Tears have stained the written line,
In each struggle, a sign divine.

Books have traveled far and wide,
Carrying dreams, a faithful guide.
Their wisdom flows through time and space,
In pages worn, we find our place.

As we turn each well-loved leaf,
We gather strength in moments brief.
Through worn pages, wisdom glows,
In the heart, the journey grows.

A Symphony of Scribbles

Lines collide in wild embrace,
Chaos dances in every space.
A symphony of colors bright,
Scribbles burst with pure delight.

Each stroke tells a tale untold,
A melody of thoughts unfolds.
Notes that flutter, rise, and fall,
In the rhythm, we hear the call.

Imperfect marks create the sound,
In every scribble, joy is found.
Harmony wraps around the page,
In written notes, we break the cage.

Passion spills from pens and hearts,
Creating beauty in the arts.
A canvas filled with dreams and schemes,
In every scribble, find the beams.

As the symphony begins to swell,
In chaos, we discover well.
Each scribble sings, a voice so clear,
In the noise, we hold what's dear.

Whispers of the Quill

Ink flows softly, a gentle stream,
Stories awaken, from hidden dream.
Each stroke a secret, a tale untold,
Whispers of the quill, in silence bold.

Pages turn slowly, worlds unfold,
Memories linger, treasures of gold.
Pen dances lightly, a magic spun,
In the quiet dusk, when day is done.

Thoughts take flight on feathered wings,
In the hush of night, the mind sings.
Captured in paper, a fleeting breath,
Life in each line, embracing depth.

A flicker of hope, a dash of pain,
Ink spills freely, like summer rain.
Echoes of laughter, shadows of fear,
Every word cherished, held so dear.

The quill whispers softly, a timeless friend,
In every story, beginnings don't end.
Crafting the moments, both sharp and sweet,
In the quiet corner, where souls meet.

From Thoughts to Stanzas

A thought arises, a spark of light,
It dances and twirls, within the night.
Captured in stanzas, the rhythm flows,
From thoughts to verses, a garden grows.

Words intertwine, like vine and tree,
A tapestry woven, wild and free.
Each line a heartbeat, a pulse of grace,
From whispers of dreams, a vivid lace.

Imaginations soar, on wings unbound,
In every stanza, a truth is found.
The essence of life, in letters dressed,
From thoughts to stanzas, hearts manifest.

A dance of ideas, swirling around,
The beauty of language, in love profound.
The quill dips low, in ink's embrace,
From quiet musings, we find our place.

In the solitude, thoughts become real,
A bridge of connection, we learn to feel.
From whispers of stories, a journey begins,
To shape our realities, with ink, we win.

Echoes in Every Line

In every line, a whisper stirs,
Echoes of laughter, of hopes and blurs.
Moments captured, each word a sigh,
A journey through time, where spirits fly.

The heartbeats of wisdom, resonate clear,
Tales of the past, we hold so dear.
In echoes we find, a voice so true,
Stories unravel, anew, anew.

Colors of feeling, brush strokes of pain,
In shadows and light, joy mingles with rain.
Each line a reminder, of love's sweet call,
In whispers and echoes, we rise, we fall.

Through valleys of silence, the words will roam,
In echoes, we find our way back home.
A symphony crafted, through rhythm and rhyme,
In every line, the pulse of time.

So listen closely, to the stories weave,
In whispers of hearts that dare to believe.
Echoes of dreams, in verses retain,
Life's dance and journey, the joy and pain.

The Alchemy of Words

Words like gold, in the hands of a sage,
Transforming the world, page by page.
Alchemy weaves, with a delicate touch,
Crafting connections, where thoughts mean so much.

From whispers to verses, a spell is cast,
In the cauldron of language, shadows amassed.
Every letter a potion, with meaning profound,
In the alchemy of words, new worlds are found.

The essence of being, distilled and refined,
In every expression, our souls intertwined.
Metaphors dance, like fireflies bright,
In the dark of the night, igniting the light.

With rhythm we draw, the cosmos in line,
Transmuting our thoughts into pearls that shine.
In the magic of language, we craft our fate,
The alchemy of words, we celebrate.

So raise your quill, let your spirit ignite,
In the tapestry woven, find your delight.
For in every strophe, in every refrain,
The alchemy of words will always remain.

Brushstrokes of Breath

In the quiet of dawn's first light,
Colors blend, day takes flight.
Whispers dance on the breeze,
Nature's palette, hearts at ease.

Each stroke written in the sky,
Gentle hues, a soft goodbye.
Painting dreams with every sigh,
Life flows on, like clouds nearby.

In shadows long, memories hide,
Captured moments, joy and pride.
Brushstrokes fade but never die,
Echoes linger, asking why.

With every breath, a tale unfolds,
A tapestry of colors bold.
Brush in hand, let passion stir,
In the silence, hearts confer.

Through twilight's gaze, stars will twinkle,
Each one a story, soft and crinkle.
Breath of life in every hue,
A canvas vast, both bright and blue.

Navigating the Narrative

Each path we choose, a tale in time,
Words like rivers, flow and climb.
In whispers soft, the stories mend,
Every chapter, a twist, a bend.

Pages turn with every breath,
In ink's embrace, we find our depth.
Characters arise from dreams we weave,
Lost in worlds, we believe.

With every step, a new surprise,
Through valleys low and mountains high.
In the silence, the heart will speak,
Find the truth in moments meek.

Navigating paths both dark and bright,
Finding solace in the night.
The narrative unfolds like a scroll,
Guiding us towards a common goal.

Language builds the bridges sought,
Tales of love, of battles fought.
In the echo of a whisper's call,
We gather strength, together stand tall.

Whimsy of the Written Word

In quills and ink, the magic grows,
Stories woven, the heart bestows.
With playful lines, the muses dance,
In the margins, dreams entrance.

Letters swirl in joyful flight,
Whimsy sparkles, pure delight.
Ideas blossom, colors bright,
Words can turn the dark to light.

Silly rhymes and tales untold,
Adventures forged, both brave and bold.
In every stanza, laughter rings,
The writer's heart forever sings.

A good book holds a friend so dear,
Each page a portal, drawing near.
Imagination takes the stage,
In the whimsy of every page.

Lines that twist and turn just so,
Chasing dreams wherever they go.
In the dance of pen and ink,
We lose ourselves, begin to think.

Melancholy in Metaphor

In shadows cast, where sorrows stand,
Whispers wrap like a gentle hand.
A tear drops softly on the ground,
In silence, echoes can be found.

The heart, a vessel worn and frayed,
Carries burdens, hopes delayed.
Between the lines, a hidden plea,
Search for light in memory.

Each metaphor, a fragile thread,
Weaving tales of joy and dread.
In layers thick, we peel away,
To understand the price to pay.

Through the gloom, a flicker shines,
In the darkness, love aligns.
With heavy hearts, we press on through,
Finding strength in shades of blue.

The world turns slow, yet time stands still,
In whispered hopes, reside the will.
Melancholy speaks in grace,
Inviting us to find our place.

Blossoms of Inspiration

In gardens bright, the flowers grow,
A dance of colors in sun's warm glow.
Each petal whispers tales of dreams,
Where hope and joy flow like streams.

With every breeze, the thoughts take flight,
They paint the world in shades of light.
Amidst the chaos, they find their place,
Creating beauty, a gentle grace.

From roots of courage, they rise and bloom,
Transforming sorrow, dispelling gloom.
Their fragrance lingers, sweet and pure,
A promise held, so bright and sure.

In every bud, a story lies,
The heart's desire beneath the skies.
With every bloom, a dream takes form,
In nature's arms, we are reborn.

So let us cherish, nurture each seed,
In every heart, a flower's need.
The blossoms bright will guide our way,
Inspiration's light, come what may.

The Magic of Metaphors

Words like rivers, flow and bend,
With currents strong, they twist and blend.
Each phrase a bridge, from thought to dream,
Where meanings dance, and shadows gleam.

A whisper soft, a roaring tide,
In every line, the worlds collide.
Imagery weaves a tapestry,
Of love, of loss, in wild decree.

Through tangled woods and open skies,
Metaphors reveal what truly lies.
They flicker like stars in the night,
Illuminating what feels right.

With every twist, a new refrain,
A playful spark, a gentle pain.
In simple words, profound delight,
The magic blooms in silent flight.

So let us dive in, swim the flow,
Embrace the tales that ebb and glow.
In metaphor's arms, we'll find our voice,
A symphony of heart, our choice.

Scribbles of Serenity

In quiet corners, thoughts abound,
The scribbles soft, a soothing sound.
A gentle touch upon the page,
The heart's calm song, a tranquil stage.

Each stroke a breath, a moment's peace,
With every line, the worries cease.
Words dance lightly, a soothing balm,
Creating space where spirits calm.

The ink flows freely, like a stream,
Woven with whispers, stitched with dreams.
In every curve, a story blooms,
Casting out shadows, dispelling glooms.

Through scribbles pure, the mind can roam,
Finding in chaos a sense of home.
The heart finds solace in silent strokes,
In every mark, a path invokes.

So take a pen, release the weight,
In scribbles soft, find a new fate.
Let serenity wash over you,
In artful scrawls, the soul breaks through.

The Essence of Expression

In every heartbeat, a tale unfolds,
An essence caught in vibrant folds.
Emotions painting the canvas wide,
Expressions bursting with colors inside.

Words spill forth like rivers swift,
Crafted with care, each precious gift.
In laughter's echo and silence's grace,
The essence captured, time can't erase.

Through joy and sorrow, love and strife,
Expressions weave the fabric of life.
In whispered secrets and cries that soar,
The essence of being, forevermore.

Art transforms the shadows to light,
Breathing form into the infinite night.
In every stroke, a piece of the soul,
Art's embrace, the spirit's goal.

To share our hearts, our truths, our dreams,
In every glance, the world redeems.
Embrace the essence, let it flow wide,
In every expression, there's love inside.

The Song Beneath the Surface

In quiet depths, the whispers flow,
A melody hidden, not seen by the glow.
Beneath the waves, where secrets lie,
The song of the heart sings soft to the sky.

Each note a memory, tender and bright,
Dancing with shadows, embracing the night.
The world above, a distant chime,
Yet deep within, there's rhythm and rhyme.

The ocean breathes, with ebb and tide,
Both calm and chaos, forever allied.
In every current, a story told,
Of love and loss, and treasures of old.

Listen close, let the waters swirl,
In every wave, a heartache unfurl.
The song beneath is waiting to find,
The pulse of the earth, intertwined and kind.

So dive deep, let the journey begin,
Feel the symphony, let it pour in.
For life's true essence resides down below,
In the song of the surface, where dreams softly flow.

Shadows of Inspiration

In the twilight glow, thoughts take flight,
Casting long shadows, a dance in the light.
Every silhouette, a story unfolds,
Whispers of dreams in whispers of gold.

In the corners of minds, creativity breathes,
Chasing the light that the darkness bequeaths.
Each stroke of brilliance fades in and out,
Like shadows that linger, then vanish in doubt.

But in the quiet, when all is still,
The heart finds paths that the soul can fulfill.
With every distraction that tries to constrain,
The shadows of inspiration begin to remain.

So write in the night, let the vision emerge,
Harness the echoes, let passion surge.
For in every shadow lies a spark so bright,
A beacon of hope in the stillness of night.

Embrace the unknown, let thoughts intertwine,
In the dance of shadows, let your heart shine.
For inspiration thrives where darkness often flows,
And the brightest ideas in the shadows arose.

Crafting Echoes

In the moment of silence, the echoes arise,
Carried on whispers and soft lullabies.
Each sound a memory, a promise to keep,
Crafting a tapestry, woven from sleep.

The pulse of existence can be felt in the air,
Every heartbeat records the love and the care.
From laughter to tears, in the passage of time,
Crafting the echoes, we find our own rhyme.

As footsteps imprint on the fragile earth,
The echoes remind us of purpose and worth.
For in every stride, a story rings true,
The path that we walk always leads us anew.

So gather the moments, let them unfold,
In the echoes of life, let your spirit be bold.
For crafting one's journey is a delicate art,
With echoes as brushstrokes, painting from the heart.

Let the music of life be your guiding line,
In every soft echo, let your soul shine.
For crafting echoes brings forth the light,
Of all that we cherish, our dreams taking flight.

Telling Truths with Rhyme

In verses sweet, the truths will gleam,
Unfolding softly, like a tender dream.
For every line carries weight and grace,
A rhythm of honesty that time can't erase.

With words as weapons, we fight the unknown,
In the garden of thoughts, our seeds have been sown.
Each rhyme a reflection, a mirror to see,
The truths of existence that set us all free.

From laughter to heartache, we weave it as one,
Beneath the same sky, beneath the same sun.
For in every stanza, a lesson resides,
The power of language connects and divides.

So speak with conviction, let your voice soar,
For telling the truths opens every door.
Embrace every narrative, both heavy and light,
With rhyme as your canvas, paint day and night.

In the tapestry of life, let your words entwine,
For telling truths is both sacred and fine.
With each passing verse, we journey along,
In the beauty of honesty, we all belong.

A Symphony of Stanzas

In quiet halls where echoes play,
Words dance in rhythm, come what may.
Notes of passion, soft and bright,
Creating worlds in the fading light.

Each stanza sings a different tale,
With whispers heard in every gale.
Verses weave like threads of gold,
Stories of love, adventure bold.

The chorus rises, hearts in sync,
In every word, we find a link.
A melody where silence speaks,
Promising more than language seeks.

From shadows cast on paper's sheen,
A symphony, both heard and seen.
Harmony flows, both wild and tame,
In every heartbeat, there's a name.

So let us write 'neath starlit skies,
In verses rich, our spirit flies.
A symphony that knows no end,
In every line, a timeless friend.

Cathedrals Built of Sound

In vaulted ceilings, whispers soar,
Each note a prayer, forevermore.
Hymns resound through arches wide,
In every heart, they coincide.

Voices blend like molten air,
Creating beauty, raw and rare.
Chorale of souls in sacred space,
Finding solace, a warm embrace.

The past and present intertwine,
In every echo, we define.
Moments captured, time unbound,
In cathedrals built of sound.

Awake our dreams with every hymn,
Notes carry hope that won't grow dim.
The music flows like rivers deep,
In sacred silence, we shall keep.

So join the choir, let hearts unite,
In harmony, we find our light.
Together we stand, hand in hand,
In cathedrals built upon the sand.

Breath of the Written World

Ink spills secrets on ancient page,
In every letter, wisdom sage.
Stories breathe like morning's dew,
Awakening dreams, both fresh and new.

Each paragraph a journey planned,
Vivid sights at the writer's hand.
Sentences flow like rivers wide,
Carrying truths we cannot hide.

The written word, a silent scream,
In black and white, we dare to dream.
Each chapter whispers, tales unfold,
Adventures waiting, brave and bold.

Through letters danced, our thoughts take flight,
Creating worlds from day to night.
With every pen stroke, paths we pave,
In this breath of life, we are brave.

So let us write with hearts ablaze,
In every line, the soul's own gaze.
A legacy in each word we draw,
A breath of life, the world in awe.

Patterns in the Chaos

In swirling colors, truth takes shape,
Amidst the discord, pathways drape.
Fragments scattered, yet aligned,
In every chaos, patterns find.

A dance of shadows, light and dark,
In disarray, there lies a spark.
Weaving tales of joy and tears,
The tapestry of life appears.

In tangled threads, we seek the thread,
Finding meaning in words unsaid.
Each twist and turn, a marked embrace,
Patterns form in time and space.

Beneath the noise, the heart beats strong,
With every pulse, we find our song.
Clarity shines through moments fraught,
In every chaos, lessons taught.

So let us trace the lines we see,
In every fracture, we are free.
For in this dance of joy and loss,
We find the meaning, find our gloss.

Crafting Dreams in Rhymes

In the quiet night, whispers flow,
Words dance lightly, forging a glow.
Dreams take shape, in starlit beams,
Crafting hopes, weaving dreams.

With every stroke, a tale begins,
A canvas bright, where light spins.
Colors blend, and shadows play,
In this realm, I long to stay.

Rhythms pulse, as thoughts entwine,
Verses bloom, like tangled vine.
Each line a step, a path to tread,
In the heart's theater, where passions led.

Time drifts softly, as pages turn,
With every line, my spirit yearns.
A journey forged, in ink so pure,
Crafting dreams, the heart's allure.

As dawn breaks, new visions rise,
In crafted dreams, the soul flies.
Endless realms in written spells,
In the heart of stories, magic dwells.

Chasing Shadows with Ink

In dimly lit corners, secrets hide,
Chasing shadows, the heart's guide.
With every stroke, the truths awake,
Ink spills stories, my soul's mistake.

Night unveils the tales untold,
Scribbled thoughts, a heart of gold.
Images linger, hard to erase,
In the darkness, I find my place.

Moments captured in fluid lines,
Each curve a dance, where fate aligns.
Ink like shadows, deep and wild,
In every mark, the heart's denied.

Fleeting whispers haunt the page,
A haunting tune, a silent rage.
Chasing ghosts with fervent thrill,
In every shadow, I find my will.

With every hue, emotions blend,
Chasing shadows, I will not bend.
In the twilight, my heart begins,
With ink as my guide, I shed my sins.

The Story Behind the Scribble

There lies a tale beneath the ink,
A whispered dream, a gentle wink.
Behind each scribble, stories bloom,
In tangled lines, the heart finds room.

Fragments scattered, lost in thought,
The story forms, a battle fought.
Every letter holds a clue,
In pages stained, the soul breaks through.

Echoes linger in written space,
In every mark, a time and place.
Unraveled yarns, a tapestry,
The scribble speaks, it sets me free.

Hidden desires dance on the ledge,
Each stroke a promise, a timeless pledge.
The heart spills forth, in chaos and grace,
In every scribble, I find my place.

In the end, it's love I chase,
Through tangled letters, I find solace.
The story tells what words can't say,
In every scribble, I find my way.

Weaving Worlds with Metaphors

In the loom of thought, I weave with care,
Metaphors glisten, floating in air.
Each thread a vision, bright and gold,
In stories untold, new worlds unfold.

I sculpt the sky with shades of dreams,
Weaving silence into whispered seams.
Every stitch, a journey sought,
In varied hues, my heart is caught.

Mountains rise from gentle lines,
Rivers flow where meaning shines.
With every twist, a fate ignites,
In metaphor's realm, my spirit's flights.

Boundless landscapes in verses lay,
Crafting wonders along the way.
Forever spinning, the tales entwine,
Every metaphor, a glimpse divine.

In this dance, I find my voice,
Weaving worlds, my heart's rejoice.
In the tapestry of dreams so large,
With metaphors, my spirit's charge.

Fluidity of the Pen

In the quiet, thoughts flow free,
A gentle stream, wild as the sea.
With every stroke, a story's born,
Whispers of day, echoes of dawn.

Ink dances lightly, tracing dreams,
Pushing the boundaries of silent screams.
Each letter a drop of pure desire,
Fanning the flames of an inner fire.

On paper, life finds its beat,
In curves and lines, where worlds meet.
Fluid as water, bold as the sun,
With the pen in hand, all battles won.

As thoughts collide, a tapestry spins,
In the heart of the writer, true magic begins.
Each twist a journey, each dot a chance,
In the rhythm of ink, we weave and dance.

Oh, how the stories yearn to flow,
Through the fluidity of the pen's soft glow.
In every page, a life to unfold,
With vibrant colors, both warm and cold.

Breathing Life into Letters

In shadows cast by paper light,
Words awaken in gentle flight.
A breath drawn deep, a sigh released,
Letters pulse, from silence, feast.

Syllables waltz in rhythmic embrace,
Filling the void, crafting a space.
Each sentence a song, a fragrant bloom,
Piercing the silence, dispelling gloom.

With quill aglow, the heart does race,
Breathing life into every trace.
Each phrase a whisper, a soft caress,
In the vast expanse, we learn to express.

Through trials felt and joys transcended,
The ink spills truths, our pains defended.
In the tapestry woven, we find our place,
In breathing life, we find our grace.

Bold like thunder, soft like rain,
Letters embrace both joy and pain.
In the dance of ink, we learn to weave,
A story alive, a dream to believe.

Celestial Verses Unveiled

Beneath the stars, ink spills its light,
Crafting verses that sparkle at night.
Galaxies swirl in poetic lines,
Whispers of cosmos in written signs.

Each word a star, each line a path,
Mapping the universe, capturing wrath.
Celestial dances in every refrain,
Names of the heavens etched in our veins.

The moon, she listens, the sun, he glows,
In open hearts, the universe flows.
Scribbles of love, of loss, of grace,
In this heavenly script, we find our place.

With ink like stardust, we craft the night,
Shape our dreams by the soft starlight.
Verses unfurl like wings in the dark,
Celestial echoes ignite a spark.

Unveiling the night, we pen our fate,
Each stroke a journey, a love innate.
In the vast expanse where our souls sail,
We find our truth in celestial tales.

Ink-stained Journeys

Steps on paper, journeys unfold,
With ink-stained dreams, brave and bold.
Every mark a path, a sight unseen,
With whispers of places we have been.

Lines like rivers, contours of fate,
With every letter, we contemplate.
The ink our compass, the page our map,
Guiding us through the world's grand gap.

In every journey, stories are found,
Ink stains the heart, where memories abound.
Colors of life merge in each hue,
In the tapestry woven, we start anew.

From mountain highs to valley dear,
Each ink-stained page holds laughter and fear.
Through deserts wide and oceans deep,
In the tales we write, our souls we keep.

With every syllable, horizons expand,
In journeys of ink, we take a stand.
Charting the unknown, together we roam,
In these ink-stained journeys, we find our home.

Colors of Expression

Red speaks of passion, bold and bright,
Blue whispers calm under starlit night.
Yellow dances with a joyful spark,
Green breathes life where shadows embark.

Orange ignites with warmth and cheer,
Violet dreams in twilight clear.
Each hue a story waiting to unfold,
A tapestry of feelings, brave and bold.

In this palette, emotions blend,
With every stroke, new worlds ascend.
Through art we share what words can't convey,
A vivid canvas, come what may.

Let colors speak where silence dwells,
In vibrant swirls, our truth compels.
Through shades and tones, we weave our tale,
In colors bright, we will not pale.

So dive into the hues of life,
Embrace the joy, the pain, the strife.
For in this spectrum, we find our way,
In colors of expression, we boldly stay.

Labors of Literary Love

Ink flows like rivers from pen to page,
Crafting dreams, setting hearts ablaze.
Pages flutter like wings unfurled,
In the solitude, a new world swirled.

Words dance lightly, a lover's embrace,
Tales of longing in every space.
Characters whisper secrets untold,
In the quiet, their stories unfold.

From dusk till dawn, the writer toils,
In ink-stained hands, the passion boils.
Each sentence a seed, each chapter a flame,
In the garden of language, love is the same.

Through struggle and strife, the muse may hide,
But the heart's longing will not abide.
With every draft, we find our voice,
In literary love, we make our choice.

The magic of words, a timeless embrace,
In the labyrinth of thoughts, we find our place.
For each book we write, a piece of our soul,
In labors of love, we are made whole.

Echoes of Elegance

In a soft whisper, the dusk descends,
Nature's breath, where beauty blends.
Rivers glide with a gentle grace,
Under the moon, they find their place.

Petals fall like sweet refrains,
Dancing lightly on silken lanes.
A waltz of shadows, a ballet profound,
In quiet corners, elegance is found.

Time flows slow, in a tender embrace,
Moments linger, each one a trace.
Reflections shimmer on still waters clear,
In echoes of elegance, we draw near.

With each heartbeat, a symphony plays,
Notes of delight in delicate ways.
The world adorned in a soft, gentle light,
In these precious echoes, the heart takes flight.

So let us savor what beauty brings,
In the art of living, elegance sings.
For in each breath, a story we weave,
In echoes of elegance, we believe.

The Whispering of Pages

Old tomes rest on shelves of time,
Their faded spines tell tales sublime.
With gentle hands, we turn each leaf,
In silent words, we find relief.

The scent of paper, a sweet perfume,
As dreams awaken from every room.
In whispers soft, the stories plead,
To journey forth, to plant a seed.

Ink-stained memories, ghosts of the past,
In every volume, shadows are cast.
Where lovers meet and heroes dare,
In the whispering pages, there's magic to share.

With every chapter, new worlds arise,
In the quiet, beneath the skies.
Through written words, our spirits soar,
In the whispering of pages, we explore.

So hold a book, feel its embrace,
In the stories told, we find our place.
For in each tale, a piece of our hearts,
In the whispering of pages, adventure starts.

Chiseling Shadows with Light

In the quiet of dawn's embrace,
Shadows dance, seeking their place.
With each ray that breaks the night,
We chisel away, crafting light.

Every gleam, a story told,
In the silence, hearts unfold.
A sculptor's hand, the sun's warm glow,
Turns dark to bright, as colors flow.

Illuminated paths we tread,
Where whispers of hope gently spread.
Each flicker, a promise, boldly cast,
Illuminating futures, breaking past.

With every beam that graces skin,
We find the strength to rise again.
Chiseling shadows, bold and free,
Light our guide, eternally.

In the dance of dusk, we see,
The fleeting essence of what can be.
Crafting dreams with every sight,
Chiseling shadows with pure light.

The Language of Dreams

In whispers soft, the night begins,
A tapestry of hopes and spins.
Each thought a thread, each wish a seam,
Woven together in the language of dreams.

Beneath the stars, our minds take flight,
In realms unbound, past wrong and right.
Echoes of laughter, tales to share,
In the quiet corners, hearts laid bare.

Night's gentle breath, a canvas wide,
Where shadows and visions intertwine and glide.
Each dream a mirror, reflecting desire,
Stoking the flames of an inner fire.

In silence we find the words unspoken,
In every dream, a promise woven.
Stories arise from the depths of night,
The language of dreams, pure and bright.

Awake and aware, in daylight's beam,
We carry the courage from each dream.
Translating whispers into the light,
The language of dreams, our guiding flight.

Weaving Winds of Inspiration

In the tapestry of morning glow,
Winds of change begin to flow.
Threads of thought in breezes blend,
Weaving inspiration, a joyful trend.

With every gust, a whisper strays,
Carrying hopes on zephyr's ways.
Golden rays and silver streams,
Infuse our hearts with vibrant dreams.

The rustling leaves sing melodies clear,
Echoing visions we hold dear.
In nature's grasp, we find our muse,
Weaving winds, the path we choose.

Through every storm, we seek the light,
Finding strength with every height.
Inspired by the swirling air,
We rise above, beyond despair.

With open hands, we catch the breeze,
In every gust, our spirits seize.
Weaving winds, a dance of grace,
Inspiration found in every place.

Crafting Light with Ink

With pen in hand, the world unfolds,
Crafting light in stories told.
Each stroke a spark, igniting soul,
With ink, we weave, becoming whole.

Words like stars in a midnight sky,
Shining bright, as hopes fly high.
An artist's heart, a flowing stream,
Crafting light from every dream.

On paper wide, our tunes resound,
In every phrase, new worlds abound.
Stories brave, with courage linked,
In our hands, we craft with ink.

Reflection of our inner fight,
Turning darkness into light.
Each letter dances, each word sings,
Crafting tales on paper wings.

With vivid hues, emotions blend,
Creating pathways that never end.
Through ink and love, we shape the night,
Crafting visions, crafting light.

Ink and Imagination

In the cauldron of thought, ideas brew,
Colors of dreams dance, vibrant and true.
With every stroke of the pen, worlds ignite,
Boundless creations take graceful flight.

Strokes of darkness, hues of bright,
Ink spills secrets, a whimsical sight.
In every drop lies a tale untold,
Imagination soars, fearless and bold.

Pages whisper of adventures unseen,
In realms of passion, where hearts convene.
From parchment to sky, the stories flow,
A river of dreams, in currents aglow.

With every word, a spell is cast,
Timeless echoes of shadows past.
Ink is the key to realms afar,
Mapping the path to where wonders are.

Dancing between the lines of lore,
Ink spills magic, forevermore.
In the heart of the writer, a spark burns bright,
Creating life from the quiet night.

Verses in the Shadows

In the corners where silence sways,
Whispers of secrets fill the bays.
Ghosts of verses, softly creep,
In the shadows, they gently seep.

A flicker of light where the dark unfolds,
Tales of the unseen that darkness holds.
Each line a heartbeat, each word a sigh,
Echoes of dreams that never die.

Murmurs of longing, soft and low,
Veils of dusk where soft winds blow.
In the quiet, shadows blend,
Verse upon verse, stories transcend.

Moonlit whispers dance on the page,
Capturing spirits, a timeless age.
In the hush of night, verses arise,
Filling the void beneath starry skies.

The ink flows like shadows in flight,
Carving the contours of the night.
In every pause, a story hides,
Verses with shadows, where magic abides.

Whispers of the Quill

In the silence, the quill starts to speak,
Whispers of thoughts, both gentle and meek.
Each stroke a promise, a tale unfolds,
From the heart of the writer, a treasure holds.

Dancing on parchment, in rhythmic flow,
Quill paints emotions, a vibrant glow.
Secrets shared between ink and hand,
Crafting a realm where dreams expand.

With whispered words, the quill takes flight,
Bringing forth visions of day and night.
In the quiet, the magic begins,
A symphony where every heart spins.

Filling the air with lyrical grace,
Every line a moment, a sacred space.
In the dance of the quill, stories intertwine,
Binding the souls through rhythm and rhyme.

From ink's tender kiss, life emerges anew,
Whispers of wisdom, a world to construe.
In every curve, a hidden delight,
The quill gives voice to the silent night.

Alchemy of Words

In the potion of language, magic brews,
Transforming thoughts into vibrant hues.
Words are the alchemists, a spark divine,
Turning the mundane into the sublime.

Every syllable carries a weight,
Cast within verses, we communicate.
With a flick of the pen, reality bends,
Words weave destinies, where each journey ends.

In shadows of silence, ideas conspire,
Alchemy of thoughts sets hearts on fire.
Metaphors simmer, awaiting their chance,
In the cauldron of ink, they gracefully dance.

Phrases emerge, like gold in the night,
Catching the dreams that take their flight.
With every word, a potion we brew,
Alchemy of life sewn through and through.

In the heart of the writer, magic ignites,
Words transform worlds, as day turns to night.
In this alchemical dance, we'll find a way,
To capture the essence of dreams that play.

Printed in the USA
CPSIA information can be obtained
at www.ICGtesting.com
LVHW020808170924
791295LV00003B/162